The Book of

UNCOMMON
PRAYER

Also by Katherine Mosby

Private Altars

The Book of

UNCOMMON
PRAYER

KATHERINE MOSBY

HarperSanFrancisco
An Imprint of HarperCollins*Publishers*

▨ A TREE CLAUSE BOOK

HarperSanFrancisco and the author, in association with The
Basic Foundation, a not-for-profit organization whose primary
mission is reforestation, will facilitate the planting of two trees
for every one tree used in the manufacture of this book.

HarperCollins Web Site: http://www.harpercollins.com

HarperCollins® ▩®, HarperSanFrancisco™,
and A TREE CLAUSE BOOK® are trademarks
of HarperCollins Publishers Inc.

Frontispiece: Peter Paul Rubens, *Seated Nude Youth*.
Courtesy of the Pierpont Morgan Library

FIRST EDITION

Library of Congress Cataloging-in-Publication Data
Mosby, Katherine.
The book of uncommon prayer / Katherine Mosby. — 1st ed.
ISBN 0−06−251358−3 (cloth)
1. Poetry, American.   2. Prayer—Poetry.   I. Title.
PS3563.088384B66   1996   95–23220
811'.54—dc20

96 97 98 99 00 ❖HAD 10 9 8 7 6 5 4 3 2 1

Dedicated to the memory of
Casey Finch

PREFACE

*"The Abbe Leroquais has aptly called the
Book of Hours the breviary of the laity.
And even more than the Breviary, the Book
of Hours lent itself to private devotions,
as well as to public observances."*

JOHN PLUMMER
Preface to
*The Book of Hours of
Catherine of Cleves*

B y the end of the Middle Ages, the Book of Hours was the most popular devotional book of the period. It was organized around the eight "hours" of the liturgical day: *matins, lauds, prime, terce, sext, none, vespers,* and *compline,* which are spaced roughly three hours apart beginning between midnight and 1:00 A.M.

These illuminated manuscripts, variously composed of devotional texts, were designed to provide a simpler model for observance than the Divine Office (a complicated annual cycle of public prayer requiring clergy). The texts were tailored to reflect the particular interests and practices of the patrons as well as local customs. To this extent, it became a personalized path to a general spiritual endeavor.

By contrast, we live in an era in which many people acknowledge a need for spirituality in their lives that is not being met by traditional sources. Moreover, the language of spirituality has been debased; pressed into the service of commerce and politics, it is now freighted with associations that undermine its very intention: to help individuals shape a fuller or more satisfying connection to their spirit.

For some of us, this endeavor is an intensely personal one that resists facile pronouncements, prescriptive or didactic. The way to grace is unique and ineffable; it is more likely to be intuited than explained. Much of what attracts us to the spiritual is its mystery, its ability to elude language. It is not surprising then to find language more often getting in the way rather than showing the way. Perhaps that is why some of us more readily make a connection through the senses—a sight or smell, a piece of music or work of art. The oblique approach occasionally finds access the direct one can't.

I began this project with the idea of exploring the intersection of poetry and prayer, creating a cycle of poems as an alternative form of meditation. Poetry, because of its ability to elevate the soul and to invest the prosaic with the profound, seemed to provide a natural link, a form of prayer broad enough to include people who can't name their god.

It seems to me it is our challenge—and reward—to determine for ourselves what is held sacred, what is meant by soul, and how both can be honored.

In 1817 Keats wrote, "I am certain of nothing but the holiness of the heart's affections and the truth of the imagination." Cultivation of the soul might be as simple as listening to one's heart and examining the different moments of one's life.

Enlightenment, perhaps, is not found in a blinding bolt of lightning but rather in a series of tiny illuminations, none of which is newsworthy but all of which combine to lift the heart and widen the aperture through which we allow ourselves to view the infinite.

The Book of

UNCOMMON
PRAYER

MATINS

Deliver me to myself
that I may stop
fretting the hours in vain,
looking for what's lacking
always elsewhere and otherwise.
Let befall me the peace
which drops like wind,
suddenly, between even the slightest
folds of a linnet's wing,
between shadow and sky, the hush
like the intervals of quiet
between questions, between the calls
of crickets, the sorrows
of one season and the next,
swift and sure and sharp
as grace.

Bleach my bones

and twine my hair

when I am gone

feed my flesh to pigeons

or jackals

or the old men

who need to warm

themselves

but first grant me

this: let one day

the shadow lift

that binds

my soul to sadness.

Teach me the beauty
of my emptiness:
the white sky
not even a crow
will mark with its
jagged flight
or fierce cry.
Fill the hollows
of my ribs with wind
until they ring
like drained glasses
rubbed into song.

LAUDS

Bring the blue
light to the pale
of crumpled sheets:
bathe me in the first
warmth gathered
like a song's
unfolding thrill
that I may rise
like milkweed,
lofting up.

Stain me with the dark
of uncontrolled
desire. Smear my name
in sweat
and soiled sheets
with a hunger
that devours pride
and fills my veins
with urgency.
Twist the flames
around me
until my every limb
curses this ripe
fruit.

O fill me
fill the abandoned
rooms
where my losses
gather to lament. No longer
thin my blood
or drain the color
from my hair for want.
In the half-light
of love grown lambent
I can almost see
a way to him
whose love
is lacking.

PRIME

Hone my gaze
to the riches
of detail—
slight as the fur
on a bee's belly
or the veins, thin as breath,
lining a forgotten iris
translucent
as a wing—
rewards
the hasty eye
and anxious heart
do not recognize.

Let sing the bedsprings
the choirboys
and mating cats.
Ring all the bells
and raise the blinds:
Let this feeling
overflow
and swell the room
with light.

Save me
from the doubts
that swarm
like maggots
feeding on a wound.
Leave me not
alone and raw
gnawed down
to the nakedness
of bone.

TERCE

See me as I am
this world
of broken buttons
and wretchedness
of words
that spark and fade
before a saw-toothed
aspiration chewing
the days like
a hungry dog rending
a greasy scrap.
Let me be
all this and yet
some loveliness.

Heal my impatient heart
which burns within me like a canker.
Teach me not to be annoyed
by faults which buzz
in my ears as loudly as mosquito wings.
Help me to love the small, the damaged,
the three-legged dog, without sorrow.
Fill me with understanding
as a pear tree fills with wind—
Touch my leaves, let my blooms shake down
and cover those I love with love.

Help me to laugh
with so much heart
I shake the trees
and tremble the quiet
pools. Surprise
the old carp
and warblers
with my joy.
Multiply my delights
till they surround
me like an echo
revolving
in a gorge.

SEXT

Speak my rage in the mouths
of mountains
turning words to ash
and flooding the plains
with wasted effort
sweeping aside trees
and cows and barns
in the bitters of my betrayal.
Sting the soil with loneliness
until not a shaft
of rye will rise
and paint the bright
land black
that I may blend my hide against
its ravaged contour
and disappear.

Let me not forget

the afternoons

full of long words

and leisure

when I was flush

in blessings

lolling in your swoon

so full

and light

every breeze was the lifting

of time's wing.

Hide me
in another season:
Use my shame
like a prism
to bend light
into sparks of color
this deed and that
blushing a thousand leaves
until the hills roar
with the burn of my regret
that only cold
can comfort.

NONE

Grant me hope
the measure of a mote
and my spirit
will rebound:
this love
will burnish
the air as if etched
in lightning
and my hands will clap
like thunder.

For I have come
so long without
a sign
into my path
shed moments
like the shake
of leaves
in handfuls
ripe and random,
a little grace
the comfort
of this gift.

Bless the grackle
and the upstart grass
the blinking sign
single glove
and broken-ribbed umbrella.
Bless the stoops
and leaky roofs
the cracks and alleys
filled with broken
men and glass.
Bless all the nouns
we cling to until
calm blankets us
like snow.

VESPERS

Fill the evening
with swallows
and smooth the air
with the waft of lilac
from behind a wall
for even anger falters
when the whole gasp
of sky is mauve
and gold are
all the windows
aflame.

Protect me
from the undertow
of failing light,
the suck of wind
lifting the last
starlings from the field
leaving nothing
but crickets
and the smooth embrace
of black.

Angels have I none
nor hope enough
to fill this length of day
yet will my heart
rush
at a swell of geese
arising
and the bells
dispersing evensong
like smoke
in the thickening air.

COMPLINE

Slake my longing
this heavy thirsting heart
with draughts and draughts
of him
until the familiar burn
and bruise is cooled
as if by marble met
or deep in earth
the damp of darkness
leaching from my skin
the lingering fever
so I may sleep again.

Still this fear
more loyal than
a friend
that I may wake
without the crease
of hard dreams
pressed into my flesh
or the trace of brine
when I swallow
and glass
in every breath.

THE PHOENIX PRAYER

A gentle stirring
like flutters
of birds
filling the garden
like vowels
swelling in the mouth
tentative kisses
these unfinished prayers:
Do not break my heart.

ACKNOWLEDGMENTS

My thanks to Kathy Anderson, Jamie Bernstein,
Nina Bernstein, Anne Cherry, Kandace Hawkinson,
Gary Hellman, and Michele Sutter.

ABOUT THE AUTHOR

Katherine Mosby is a poet and novelist.
She teaches writing courses and conducts poetry
workshops in New York City and is the author
of the acclaimed novel *Private Altars*.

The Book of Uncommon Prayer is set in Bembo, a typeface based on an original cut by Francesco Griffo. Bembo was first used in 1495 by printer-publisher Aldus Manutius for *De Aetna* by Cardinal Bembo, whom the modern version is named after.

Printing by Haddon Craftsmen, Inc.
Book design by Ralph Fowler